Table of Contents:

Section 1: Tracking Income and Expenses
 - Gathering financial documents
 - Categorizing expenses
 - Recording income and expenses
 - Reviewing and analyzing spending

Section 2: Creating and Following a Budget
 - Determining income
 - Listing expenses
 - Setting financial goals
 - Allocating income
 - Tracking progress

Section 3: Saving and Building an Emergency Fund
 - Setting savings goals
 - Automating savings
 - Cutting expenses
 - Saving windfalls and bonuses
 - Building an emergency fund

Section 4: Paying off Debts and Avoiding Bad Debts
 - Evaluating debts
 - Prioritizing high-interest debts
 - Using debt repayment strategies
 - Avoiding bad debts

Chapter 3: The Principles of Investing

Section 1: Understanding Different Types of Investments
1.1 Stocks

1.2 Bonds
1.3 Mutual Funds
1.4 Exchange-Traded Funds (ETFs)
1.5 Real Estate
1.6 Commodities
1.7 Options and Futures

Section 2: Diversifying Your Portfolio and Reducing Risk
2.1 Asset Allocation
2.2 Geographic Diversification
2.3 Sector Diversification
2.4 Rebalancing

Section 3: Choosing the Best Investment Strategy
3.1 Buy and Hold
3.2 Value Investing
3.3 Growth Investing
3.4 Income Investing

Chapter 4: The Secrets of Income Generation

Section 1: Increasing Income from Your Current Job or Career
1. Evaluate Your Skills and Knowledge
2. Seek Additional Responsibilities
3. Enhance Your Network
4. Demonstrate Exceptional Performance

Section 2: Negotiating Your Salary and Benefits
1. Research Market Salaries
2. Highlight Your Value
3. Be Flexible

4. Practice Effective Communication

Section 3: Creating Multiple Streams of Income
1. Identify Your Skills and Passions
2. Explore Freelancing or Consulting
3. Invest in Income-Generating Assets
4. Develop a Side Business or Online Venture

Section 4: Starting and Growing a Profitable Business or Side Hustle
1. Conduct Market Research
2. Develop a Business Plan
3. Secure Financing or Funding
4. Implement Effective Marketing Strategies
5. Monitor and Adjust Your Business Growth

Chapter 5: The Strategies of Wealth Protection

1. Protecting Assets and Income from Taxes, Inflation, and Lawsuits
    1.1 Tax Planning
    1.2 Asset Diversification
    1.3 Trusts and Asset Protection Entities
    1.4 Insurance Coverage

2. Insuring Yourself and Your Family against Unexpected Events
    2.1 Life Insurance
    2.2 Health Insurance
    2.3 Disability Insurance
    2.4 Long-Term Care Insurance

3. Planning for Retirement and Estate

Chapter 6: Bonus

Welcome to My e-book on how to create wealth and become rich. My name is Richard Mugumya. If you've ever wondered if financial success and freedom are within your reach, regardless of your background or starting point, the answer is a resounding yes. In this e-book, we will delve into the principles and strategies that can empower you to build Welcome to this e-book on how to create wealth and become rich. If you've ever wondered if financial success and freedom are within your reach, regardless of your background or starting point, the answer is a resounding yes. In this e-book, we will delve into the principles and strategies that can empower you to build wealth and achieve your financial goals over time.

Within these virtual pages, we will address the common obstacles and challenges that often hinder individuals from attaining their financial aspirations. Whether your dreams involve early retirement, purchasing your dream home, exploring the world, or leaving a lasting legacy for your loved ones, this e-book will equip you with the knowledge to embark on your journey towards wealth and riches.

So, are you ready to unlock the secrets of financial success and learn how to get rich? Together, we will explore the strategies and mindset shifts that will set you on a path to financial abundance. Let's dive in and discover the possibilities that lie ahead.

Forget about get-rich-quick schemes or exclusive secrets known only to a privileged few. The methods we'll explore here are proven and accessible to everyone, regardless of income, education, or background. By the end of this eBook, you will gain a deeper understanding of how money works, master financial management, make wise investments, boost your income, and protect your assets.

Chapter 1: The Mindset of Wealth

Introduction:

The mindset of wealth plays a crucial role in achieving financial success and abundance. It involves developing a positive and abundant mindset, overcoming limiting beliefs and fears, setting smart and realistic financial goals, and cultivating gratitude and generosity. In this chapter, we will explore each of these aspects in detail and provide practical strategies to help you cultivate a mindset of wealth.

Section 1: Developing a Positive and Abundant Mindset

1. Understand the Power of Your Thoughts:

Recognize that your thoughts shape your reality. By consciously choosing positive and empowering thoughts, you can create a mindset that attracts abundance and success.

2. Practice Positive Self-Talk:

Replace negative self-talk with affirmations and positive statements. Repeat empowering affirmations daily to rewire your subconscious mind and reinforce positive beliefs about wealth and abundance.

3. Surround Yourself with Positive Influences:

Associate with people who have a positive and abundant mindset. Surrounding yourself with individuals who are motivated, supportive, and successful can inspire and uplift you on your journey.

Section 2: Overcoming Limiting Beliefs and Fears

1. Identify Your Limiting Beliefs:

Reflect on the beliefs that may be holding you back from achieving financial success. Common limiting beliefs include "money is evil" or "I don't deserve wealth." Awareness is the first step toward overcoming these beliefs.

2. Challenge and Reframe Limiting Beliefs:

Question the validity of your limiting beliefs and replace them with empowering beliefs. For example, if you believe that "money is evil," reframe it as "money allows me to make a positive impact in the world."

3. Take Action despite Fear:

Fear of failure or success can paralyze you. Understand that fear is a natural response to stepping out of your comfort zone. Take small, manageable steps toward your goals, gradually expanding your comfort zone and building confidence.

Section 3: Setting Smart and Realistic Financial Goals

1. Define Your Long-Term Vision:

Clarify your long-term financial goals and aspirations. Visualize your ideal financial future and create a compelling vision that will motivate and guide you.

2. Break Down Goals into Smaller Milestones:

Divide your long-term goals into smaller, achievable milestones. This approach allows you to track progress, celebrate achievements, and maintain momentum.

3. Make Goals Specific, Measurable, Attainable, Relevant, and Time-Bound (SMART):

Ensure that your goals are SMART. They should be specific, measurable, attainable, relevant, and time bound. This framework provides clarity and increases the likelihood of success.

Section 4: Cultivating Gratitude and Generosity

1. Practice Daily Gratitude:

Develop a habit of expressing gratitude for the abundance in your life. Regularly acknowledge and appreciate the financial resources, opportunities, and relationships you have.

2. Give Freely and Generously:

Cultivate a mindset of generosity by giving back to others. This can be through charitable donations, volunteering, or simply acts of kindness. Sharing cocreate resources and creates a positive flow of abundance in your life.

3. Embrace Abundance Mentality:

Shift from a scarcity mentality to an abundance mentality. Recognize that there is enough wealth and opportunities for everyone. Embracing abundance allows you to attract more prosperity into your life.

Developing a mindset of wealth is a transformative journey that requires consistent effort and self-reflection. By cultivating a positive and abundant mindset, overcoming.

Chapter 2: The Basics of Money Management

Section 1: Tracking Income and Expenses

Tracking your income and expenses is a fundamental step in effective money management. It allows you to understand where your money is coming from and where it's going. Here are some steps to help you track your income and expenses:

1. Gather your financial documents:

Collect all your income statements, bank statements, credit card statements, and receipts.

2. Categorize your expenses:

Create categories for your expenses, such as housing, transportation, groceries, utilities, entertainment, etc. This will help you analyze your spending patterns.

3. Record your income and expenses:
Use a spreadsheet, budgeting software, or a smartphone app to record your income and expenses regularly. Be diligent and track all your transactions.

4. Review and analyze your spending:

Periodically review your spending patterns. Identify areas where you're overspending and find opportunities for saving.

Section 2: Creating and Following a Budget

Creating a budget is crucial for managing your finances effectively. It helps you allocate your income towards different expenses and savings goals. Follow these steps to create and follow a budget:

1. Determine your income:

Calculate your total monthly income, including salary, freelance income, and any other sources.

2. List your expenses:

Make a comprehensive list of all your monthly expenses, including fixed expenses (rent/mortgage, utilities) and variable expenses (groceries, entertainment).

3. Set financial goals:

 Identify your short-term and long-term financial goals. These could include saving for a vacation, paying off debt, or building an emergency fund.

4. Allocate your income:

Assign a portion of your income to each expense category and savings goal. Ensure that your expenses do not exceed your income.

5. Track your progress:

Continuously monitor your spending against your budget. Adjust as needed and hold yourself accountable for sticking to your plan.

Section 3: Saving and Building an Emergency Fund

Saving money and building an emergency fund are essential for financial stability and preparedness. Follow these steps to save effectively:

1. Set savings goals:

Determine how much you want to save each month and set specific savings goals, such as saving 10% of your income.

2. Automate your savings:

Set up automatic transfers from your checking account to a savings account. This makes saving a consistent habit.

3. Cut expenses:

Identify areas where you can reduce your spending and redirect those funds towards savings. It could be as simple as cutting down on dining out or canceling unused subscriptions.

4. Save windfalls and bonuses:

Whenever you receive unexpected money, such as tax refunds or work bonuses, save a portion of it instead of spending it all.

5. Build an emergency fund:

Aim to save at least three to six months' worth of living expenses in an emergency fund. This will provide a financial safety net in case of unexpected events.

Section 4: Paying off Debts and Avoiding Bad Debts

Managing and paying off debts is crucial for maintaining a healthy financial life. Here's how to approach debt management:

1. Evaluate your debts:

Make a list of all your debts, including the outstanding balances, interest rates, and minimum monthly payments.

2. Prioritize high-interest debts:

Focus on paying off high-interest debts first, as they cost you more in the long run. Make minimum payments on other debts while putting extra money towards the high-interest ones.

Chapter 3: The Principles of Investing

Section 1: Understanding Different Types of Investments

When it comes to investing, there are various types of investments you can consider. Understanding these different types is crucial in building a well-diversified portfolio. Here are some common investment options:

1. Stocks:

Stocks represent ownership shares in a company. When you buy stocks, you become a shareholder and have the potential to earn returns through dividends and capital appreciation.

2. Bonds:

Bonds are debt instruments issued by governments, municipalities, or corporations to raise capital. When you buy a bond, you are essentially lending money to the issuer in exchange for regular interest payments and the return of the principal amount at maturity.

3. Mutual Funds:

Mutual funds pool money from multiple investors to invest in a diversified portfolio of stocks, bonds, or other assets. They are managed by professional fund managers.

4. Exchange-Traded Funds (ETFs):

ETFs are like mutual funds but trade on stock exchanges like individual stocks. They offer diversification and can track various market indices or sectors.

5. Real Estate:

Investing in real estate involves purchasing properties or real estate investment trusts (REITs) that generate rental income or appreciate over time.

6. Commodities:

Commodities include physical goods like gold, oil, or agricultural products. Investors can trade commodities directly or invest in commodity-based funds.

7. Options and Futures:

Options and futures are derivative instruments that derive their value from an underlying asset. They are often used for hedging or speculation.

Section 2: Diversifying Your Portfolio and Reducing Risk

Diversification is a strategy that involves spreading your investments across different asset classes, industries, and geographic regions to reduce risk. Here's how you can diversify your portfolio:

1. Asset Allocation:

Allocate your investments across different asset classes (e.g., stocks, bonds, real estate) based on your risk tolerance, investment goals, and time horizon. A well-diversified portfolio typically includes a mix of assets.

2. Geographic Diversification:

Invest in companies or assets from different countries and regions to reduce exposure to specific economic or political risks.

3. Sector Diversification:

Spread your investments across various industry sectors (e.g., technology, healthcare, finance) to avoid concentration in a single sector.

4. Rebalancing:

Regularly review and rebalance your portfolio to maintain the desired asset allocation. This involves selling over-performing assets and buying under-performing ones to bring your portfolio back in line with your target allocation.

Section 3: Choosing the Best Investment Strategy

Choosing the right investment strategy depends on your financial goals, risk tolerance, and time horizon. Here are a few strategies to consider:

1. Buy and Hold:

This strategy involves buying investments with a long-term perspective and holding them regardless of short-term market fluctuations. It requires patience and discipline.

2. Value Investing:

Value investors look for undervalued assets with the belief that their true value will be recognized over time. They focus on fundamentals like earnings, assets, and cash flow.

3. Growth Investing:

Growth investors seek companies with the potential for above-average growth. They prioritize earnings growth, market share, and innovation.

4. Income Investing:

Income investors aim to generate a steady stream of income from their investments. They often focus on dividend-paying stocks, bonds, or real estate investment trusts (REITs).

Chapter 4: The Secrets of Income Generation

In this chapter, we will explore strategies and techniques for increasing your income from your current job or career, negotiating your salary and benefits, creating multiple streams of income, as well as starting and growing a profitable business or side hustle. By implementing these secrets, you can take control of your financial future and achieve your income goals.

Section 1: Increasing Income from Your Current Job or Career

1. Evaluate Your Skills and Knowledge:

Identify areas where you can improve your skills and knowledge to become more valuable to your employer. Take courses, attend workshops, or pursue professional certifications to enhance your expertise.

2. Seek Additional Responsibilities:

Take the initiative to ask for more responsibilities at work. Volunteer for challenging projects or tasks that align with your skills and interests. By demonstrating your capabilities, you increase your chances of earning promotions or salary raises.

3. Enhance Your Network:

Build strong relationships with colleagues, managers, and industry professionals. Attending networking events, joining professional organizations, and engage in online communities. Your network can provide valuable opportunities for career advancement and income growth.

4. Demonstrate Exceptional Performance:

Strive for excellence in your current role. Consistently deliver high-quality work, exceed targets, and go above and beyond expectations. By demonstrating your value to the company, you increase your chances of receiving performance-based bonuses or raises.

Section 2: Negotiating Your Salary and Benefits

1. Research Market Salaries:

Before entering negotiations, research salary ranges for similar positions in your industry and location. Websites like Glassdoor, pay scale, or industry-specific salary surveys can provide valuable information. This knowledge will empower you to negotiate from an informed position.

2. Highlight Your Value:

During negotiations, emphasize your skills, experience, and accomplishments that make you an asset to the company. Clearly articulate the value you bring and how it positively impacts the organization's bottom line.

3. Be Flexible:

Consider negotiating beyond just base salary. Explore other benefits such as bonuses, stock options, flexible work arrangements, additional vacation days, or professional development opportunities. Sometimes, non-monetary benefits can significantly enhance your overall compensation package.

4. Practice Effective Communication:

Develop strong negotiation and communication skills. Be confident, articulate, and assertive while maintaining a professional and respectful tone. Clearly express your expectations and actively listen to the employer's perspective.

Section 3: Creating Multiple Streams of Income

1. Identify Your Skills and Passions:

Determine your areas of expertise and areas that genuinely interest you. Look for opportunities to leverage these skills outside of your primary job.

2. Explore Freelancing or Consulting:

Consider offering your services as a freelancer or consultant in your field. Freelancing platforms like Upwork or Fiverr can connect you with potential clients. This way, you can earn additional income by taking on projects in your spare time.

3. Invest in Income-Generating Assets:

Explore investment opportunities such as stocks, bonds, real estate, or starting an investment portfolio. These assets can generate passive income over time, diversifying your income sources.

4. Develop a Side Business or Online Venture:

Capitalize on your entrepreneurial spirit by starting a side business or online venture. Identify a niche market or a problem you can solve and develop a business plan. Leverage online platforms, social media, and e-commerce to reach a broader customer base.

Chapter 5: The Strategies of Wealth Protection

In this chapter, we will explore various strategies to protect your assets and income from taxes, inflation, and lawsuits. We will also discuss how to insure yourself and your family against unexpected events, plan for your retirement and estate, as well as how to donate and share your wealth with others. Let's delve into these topics:

1. Protecting Assets and Income from Taxes, Inflation, and Lawsuits:

a. **Tax Planning:**
Work with a qualified tax professional to identify legal strategies to minimize your tax liability, such as taking advantage of tax deductions, credits, and exemptions.

b. **Asset Diversification:**
Invest in a variety of asset classes, such as stocks, bonds, real estate, and commodities, to reduce the risk of losing wealth due to inflation or economic downturns.

c. **Trusts and Asset Protection Entities:**
Consider setting up trusts or asset protection entities to shield your assets from potential lawsuits and creditors.

d. **Insurance Coverage:**
Obtain adequate insurance coverage, including liability insurance, to protect against potential financial losses resulting from lawsuits or unexpected events.

2. Insuring Yourself and Your Family against Unexpected Events:

a. **Life Insurance:**
Purchase life insurance policies to provide financial support for your family in the event of your untimely death.

b. **Health Insurance:**
Secure comprehensive health insurance coverage for yourself and your family to mitigate the financial burden of medical expenses.

c. **Disability Insurance:**
Consider disability insurance to replace lost income if you are unable to work due to illness or injury.

d. **Long-Term Care Insurance:**
Plan for potential long-term care needs by obtaining long-term care insurance to cover expenses associated with nursing homes, assisted living, or in-home care.

3. *Planning for Retirement and Estate*:

a. **Retirement Savings:**
Save diligently for retirement through retirement accounts such as 401(k)s, IRAs, or pension plans.

b. **Estate Planning:**
Consult with an estate planning attorney to create a comprehensive estate plan that includes a will, trusts, and powers of attorney to ensure your assets are distributed according to your wishes.

c. **Succession Planning:**
If you own a business, develop a succession plan to facilitate a smooth transition of ownership when you retire or in the event of unforeseen circumstances.

4. Donating and Sharing Your Wealth with Others:

a. **Charitable Giving:**
   Consider donating a portion of your wealth to charitable organizations to support causes you care about while potentially obtaining tax benefits.

b. **Family Gifting:**
   Strategically gift assets to family members to reduce your taxable estate and provide financial assistance to loved ones.

c. **Philanthropic Vehicles:**
   Explore philanthropic vehicles such as donor-advised funds or private foundations to create a structured approach to charitable giving while maintaining control over the distribution of funds.

Remember, the strategies mentioned here are general considerations, and it's crucial to consult with financial professionals, attorneys, and tax advisors who can provide personalized guidance based on your specific circumstances and goals.

Conclusion:

In this e-book, we have explored a range of strategies to protect your wealth, assets, and income. By implementing these strategies, you can safeguard your financial well-being, ensure a secure future for yourself and your loved ones, and even make a positive impact on others.

Throughout the chapters, we discussed the importance of tax planning, asset diversification, and the use of trusts and asset protection entities to shield your assets from potential risks. We also emphasized the significance of adequate insurance coverage to protect against unexpected events and the value of planning for retirement and estate to secure a comfortable future. Furthermore, we explored the power of charitable giving and sharing your wealth to make a difference in the world.

However, it is crucial to remember that every individual's financial situation is unique. The strategies presented in this e-book serve as a starting point, but it is essential to seek personalized advice from financial professionals, attorneys, and tax advisors who can tailor the strategies to your specific needs and circumstances.

By taking a proactive approach to wealth protection, you can gain peace of mind knowing that your hard-earned assets and income are shielded from taxes, inflation, and potential lawsuits. You can also create a legacy that extends beyond financial success by donating and sharing your wealth with others.

Remember, wealth protection is an ongoing process that requires regular review and adjustment as your circumstances evolve. Stay informed, stay diligent, and continue to educate yourself about financial planning and wealth management to ensure a prosperous and secure future.

Thank you for reading this e-book, and we wish you success in implementing the strategies outlined herein. Here's to your financial security, peace of mind, and a legacy of generosity and impact!

Chapter 6: Bonus

This is your bonus for not giving up on your dreams. Please continue reading: <u>Placements</u>

Placements refer to the platforms or channels where the e-book can be made available for readers to access and purchase. Here are some potential placements for your e-book:

1. Online Marketplaces:
Publish your e-book on popular online marketplaces such as Amazon Kindle Direct Publishing (KDP), Barnes & Noble Nook Press, Apple Books, or Google Play Books. These platforms have a wide reach and allow readers to purchase and download eBooks for various devices.

2. Your website or Blog:

If you have a website or blog focused on personal finance or wealth management, consider offering the e-book as a digital download directly from your site. This allows you to retain control over distribution and potentially capture leads for future marketing efforts.

3. Social Media Platforms:

Leverage social media platforms like Facebook, Instagram, Twitter, or LinkedIn to promote your e-book and provide links to purchase or download. You can create engaging posts, share excerpts, and run targeted ads to reach your desired audience.

4. Email Marketing:

If you have an email list or newsletter subscribers, utilize email marketing to promote your e-book directly to your audience. Craft compelling email campaigns that highlight the value and benefits of the e-book and include a call-to-action to purchase or download.

5. Collaboration with Influencers or Bloggers:

Collaborate with influencers or bloggers in the personal finance or wealth management niche who have an engaged audience. Offer them a free copy of your e-book in exchange for honest reviews or guest blog posts that promote your e-book.

6. Podcasts and Webinars:

If you have your own podcast or participate as a guest on relevant podcasts, promote your e-book to the podcast audience. Additionally, consider hosting webinars or workshops where you can share valuable insights from the e-book and provide a link for attendees to purchase or download it.

Remember to tailor your marketing efforts to the specific placements you choose. Each platform may require different marketing strategies and tactics to effectively reach your target audience and drive e-book sales or downloads.

General principles and strategies

Creating wealth and becoming rich is a multifaceted goal that requires a combination of mindset, knowledge, and strategic actions. While there is no guaranteed formula for success, here are some general principles and strategies that can help you on your path to wealth creation:

1. Develop a Wealth Mindset:

Cultivate a mindset that embraces abundance, opportunity, and financial success. Believe in your ability to create wealth and be willing to take calculated risks.

2. Set Clear Financial Goals:

Define your financial goals with clarity. Establish both short-term and long-term objectives, and make sure they are specific, measurable, achievable, relevant, and time-bound (SMART goals).

3. Create a Budget and Stick to It:

A budget is a crucial tool for managing your finances effectively. Track your income, expenses, and savings meticulously. Identify areas where you can cut back on unnecessary spending and allocate more funds towards saving and investing.

4. Increase Your Income:

Look for opportunities to increase your income. This might involve asking for a raise, seeking promotions, acquiring new skills, starting a side business, or exploring investment opportunities.

5. Save and Invest Wisely:

Saving money is essential, but it's equally important to invest your savings wisely. Educate yourself about different investment options such as stocks, bonds, real estate, and mutual funds. Consider diversifying your investments to spread risk and maximize potential returns.

6. Build Multiple Streams of Income:

Relying solely on a single income source can be risky. Explore ways to diversify your income by creating multiple streams of revenue. This might involve investing in rental properties, starting an online business, or generating passive income through dividends or royalties.

7. **Control Debt: Minimize and manage your debt effectively.**

High-interest debt can drain your financial resources and limit your ability to build wealth. Prioritize paying off debts with the highest interest rates first and avoid taking on unnecessary debt whenever possible.

8. **Continuously Educate Yourself:**

Stay updated on financial trends, investment strategies, and personal finance principles. Read books, attend seminars, follow financial experts, and surround yourself with knowledgeable individuals who can guide and inspire you.

9. **Network and Build Relationships:**

Networking is valuable for both personal and professional growth. Connect with like-minded individuals, mentors, and successful people in your field of interest. Learn from their experiences, seek advice, and explore potential collaborative opportunities.

10. **Be Patient and Persistent:**

Wealth creation takes time and effort. Stay focused on your goals, remain disciplined, and be persistent in your pursuit of financial success. Embrace failures as learning experiences and adapt your strategies as needed.

Remember, becoming rich is not solely about accumulating material wealth. It's also important to find fulfillment and lead a balanced life. Prioritize your health, relationships, and personal well-being along the way.

Common themes that emerge from Millionaires and Billionaires stories:

(1) Learn from failure:

 Failure is inevitable, but it can also be a valuable source of feedback and improvement. As Bill Gates said, "It's fine to celebrate success but it is more important to heed the lessons of failure".

(2) Insist on excellence.

Excellence is not a one-time event, but a habit that requires constant effort and dedication. Mohammad Dewji, Africa's youngest billionaire, advises, "Always strive for excellence in life and never make room for mediocrity. Set your standards high and your efforts shall be rewarded."

(3) Create value for others.

The difference between a millionaire and a billionaire is not just a matter of scale, but of impact. Billionaires create products, services, and investments that benefit millions of people, not just themselves. As Steve Jobs said, "Being the richest man in the cemetery doesn't matter to me. Going to bed at night saying we've done something wonderful, that's what matters to me."

(4) Think big and act boldly.

Billionaires are not afraid to pursue audacious goals that challenge the status quo and push the boundaries of what is possible. They are also willing to take calculated risks and seize opportunities when they arise. As Elon Musk said, "When something is important enough, you do it even if the odds are not in your favor."

(5)Be frugal and smart with money.

Billionaires know how to manage their money wisely and avoid unnecessary expenses. They also invest their money in assets that generate income and growth, rather than liabilities that depreciate and drain resources. As Warren Buffett said, "Don't save what is left after spending; spend what is left after saving."

These are some of the lessons that you can learn from the lives and achievements of millionaires and Billionaires. Good Luck!

These are common mistakes that millionaires and billionaires make, according to various sources:

(1) Not diversifying their income.

Relying on one source of income can limit your potential and expose you to more risk. Many successful people create multiple streams of income, such as investing, starting a business, or creating a product.

(2) Not tracking their spending.

Spending more than you earn can quickly erode your wealth and put you in debt. It's important to track your spending and budget wisely and avoid unnecessary or impulsive purchases.

(3) Not investing early or at all.

Investing is one of the most powerful ways to grow your money over time, thanks to compound interest. However, many people miss out on this opportunity by not investing early, or not investing at all. Investing also requires research, patience, and discipline, and avoiding emotional or speculative decisions.

(4) Not being adaptable or innovative.

The world is constantly changing, and so are the needs and preferences of consumers. Millionaires and billionaires who fail to adapt or innovate can lose their competitive edge and market share. They need to be open to new ideas, feedback, and opportunities, and embrace change rather than resist it.

(5) Not living in the present.

While it's good to have a vision for the future and plan ahead, it's also important to enjoy the present and appreciate what you have. Some millionaires and billionaires regret not spending more time with their family, friends, or hobbies, or not taking care of their health and well-being.

Some of the books you should read about Millionaires and Billionaires:

(1) Shoe Dog: A Memoir by the Creator of Nike by Phil Knight.

This is a candid and inspiring memoir by the founder of Nike, who shares his journey from a start-up to a global brand. Bill Gates named it one of his five favorite books of 2016.

(2) The Millionaire Next Door: The Surprising

Secrets of America's Wealthy by Thomas J. Stanley and William D. Danko.

This is a classic book that reveals the common traits and habits of millionaires, based on extensive research and interviews. It challenges the stereotypes and myths about wealth and success.

(3) The Path Made Clear: Discovering Your Life's Direction and Purpose by Oprah Winfrey.

This is a motivational book by the media mogul and philanthropist, who shares her own story and wisdom, as well as insights from other influential people. It helps you find your passion and purpose in life.

(4) Principles: Life and Work by Ray Dalio.

This is a practical and insightful book by the founder of Bridgewater Associates, the world's largest hedge fund. It outlines the principles that Dalio used to achieve his personal and professional goals, and how you can apply them to your own challenges.

(5) The Millionaire and the Bard: Henry Folger's Obsessive Hunt for Shakespeare's First Folio by Andrea Mays.

This is a fascinating book that tells the story of Henry Folger, a millionaire oil executive who amassed the largest collection of Shakespeare's works in the world. It reveals his passion, obsession, and legacy.

These are some of the books that you can read about millionaires and billionaires. I hope you find this book interesting and you enjoyed reading it or listening in audio form. Good Luck!